EAGLES

A PORTRAIT OF THE ANIMAL WORLD

HAL H. WYSS

NEW LINE BOOKS

Fax: (888) 719-7723
e-mail: info@newlinebooks.com

Printed and bound in China

ISBN 978-1-59764-347-4

Visit us on the web!
www.newlinebooks.com

PHOTO CREDITS

Photographer/Page Number

Barry W. Barker 42 (left)

Bruce Coleman, Inc.
Kenneth Fink 42 (right)
C.B. Frith 45 (top)

E. R. Degginger 7 (bottom) 11, 47, 53 (bottom), 63, 65

Dembinsky Photo Associates
Mike Barlow 4 (bottom)
Barbara Gerlach 54
Bill Lea 6
Stan Osolinski 5, 58, 62, 66 (top)
Fritz Polking 15
Anup Shah 71
Mark J. Thomas 61
Martin Withers 37, 40–41, 55 (bottom)

Jeff Foott 20, 29

Brian Kenney 21

Tom & Pat Leeson 3, 4 (top), 7 (top), 8–9,
12, 13, 14, 16 (top & bottom), 22, 26 (bottom),
28 (top & bottom), 30, 31, 32, 33 (top & bottom),
34, 35, 48, 60 (top), 64 (bottom), 66

Nature Photographers Ltd.
Frank B. Blackburn 51
L. H. Brown 60 (bottom)
Kevin Carlson 53 (top)
Peter Craig-Cooper 67 (top), 68–69, 70
R. S. Daniell 59
Geoff Du Feu 10 (top), 64 (top)
Michael Gure 52
E. A. James 49
Roger Tidman 50 (top)

Photo Researchers, Inc.
Jose Luis Grande 50 (bottom)

Tom Stack & Associates
Nancy Adams 39
Joe McDonald 43
Mike Severns 41 (right)
Roy Toft 36
Dave Watts 45 (bottom), 46 (top & bottom)

Lynn M. Stone 19, 23, 24–25, 26 (top), 27 (top & bottom)

VIREO/Acadamy of Natural Sciences, Philadelphia
A. & S. Cary 56–57
W. S. Clark 49 (bottom)
P. Davey 38
K. Overman 55 (top)
M. Strange 44
R. Tipper 10 (bottom)

INTRODUCTION

Bald eagles feed primarily on fish and are seldom found far from water.

Throughout recorded history the eagle has been a primary symbol of grandeur, military might, and political authority. For most Americans, the eagle so revered is the bald eagle, which is often called the American eagle. Elsewhere, however, the symbolic eagle may be the white-tailed eagle of northern Europe, the imperial eagle of southern Europe, North Africa, and Asia, the martial eagle of Africa, the Philippine eagle of the Pacific, or the harpy eagle of Central and South America.

Between sixty and sixty-five species of eagles exist in the world. The exact number is dependent on whether one considers the various types of crested serpent eagles to be separate species or merely "races" within a single species, and whether a bird such as the vulturine fish eagle is better classified as an eagle or a vulture. Eagles breed on six continents—all except Antarctica—and on many of the world's larger islands. Some, such as the golden eagle (which breeds throughout the northern hemisphere), are widely distributed and maintain large populations. Others, including the Philippine eagle and Sanford's sea eagle, have tiny breeding ranges and populations numbering only in the hundreds. It is feared, in fact, that the wild population of the Philippine eagle may be extinct within a decade and that the bird will exist only in zoos.

Because eagles belong to as many as twenty-two separate biological genera, because they vary widely in size, appearance, and behavior, and because many are closely related to various kinds of hawks, it is difficult to determine what, if anything, all eagles have in common

and what characteristics separate them from other birds of prey. Perhaps the most obvious characteristic eagles share is large size. Although there is a good deal of size variation, eagles tend to be the largest birds of prey and the largest species in their various genera. Eagles are daytime hunters, and all have extraordinarily keen eyesight. In fact, we use "eagle-eyed" as a metaphor for excellent vision. Most eagles capture living prey in water, on the ground, or in trees, but seldom capture flying birds. Many eagles sometimes feed on carrion.

Exactly how large eagles grow to be and which species is largest depends on what part of the eagle is being measured. For example, the largest wingspan (over 8 feet, or 2.44 meters) is achieved by the magnificent Steller's sea eagle of eastern Siberia. In weight, the Steller's sea eagle is about the

same as the harpy eagle (between eighteen and twenty pounds), but the harpy eagle is adapted to flying among trees in rainforests and hence has stubby wings. The Steller's has the largest beak (nearly three inches in length), which it uses for tearing into the tough hides of salmon. On the other hand, the harpy preys on such mammals as two-toed sloths and howler monkeys and has absolutely enormous talons. Researchers studying the harpy at close range wear helmets and bulletproof vests as protection against talons larger than the claws of grizzly bears. Current consensus seems to give the Steller's sea eagle a slight advantage in size over the harpy eagle, with the Philippine eagle, bald eagle, golden eagle, and martial eagle not far behind.

The sixty or more species of eagles are classified into four major groups: (1) sea eagles and fish eagles; (2) large rainforest eagles; (3) booted eagles; (4) serpent and snake eagles. There are about eleven species of sea eagles and fish eagles, including the American bald eagle. These birds are mostly coastal, although some, such as Pallas's sea eagle of south central Asia, prefer inland waterways. As the name denotes, eagles of this group subsist mainly on fish and, by necessity, hunt in

The feet of a bald eagle are tipped with very sharp talons used to snare fish from the surface of lakes and rivers.

the open; hence, they are the most easily studied and observed of the groups of eagles. Sea eagles and fish eagles are found on all continents except South America and Antarctica.

Sea and fish eagles may gather in sizable numbers where there are concentrations of fish. The November run of Chum Salmon in the Chilkat River near Haines, Alaska, attracts about four thousand bald eagles annually; two hundred or more may be visible in a single photograph.

Only six species are included in the large rainforest group of eagles, but among these are two of the world's largest eagles, the harpy and the Philippine. Eagles in this group are

Wahlberg's eagle is a slim, dark, booted eagle of central Africa which feeds primarily on snakes, lizards, and small rodents.

Bald eagles are one of a number of species of eagles which mate for life and are often seen in pairs.

Following page: The wings of a soaring bald eagle appear much flatter than those of hawks and vultures, which usually have a definite upward curve.

The tawny eagle of Africa belongs to the family of booted eagles. It is one of the world's most abundant eagles.

thirty species. These birds are called "booted" because their feathers extend much farther down the leg and onto the feet than is true of other eagles. Since their toes are not feathered, these eagles are really more trousered than booted. Booted eagles are found on all continents except Antarctica and include the most populous species: the tawny and steppe eagles, with a combined population of over one million; the Australian wedge-tailed eagle, numbering 600 to 700 thousand; and the golden eagle, whose combined Asian, European, and North American populations are thought to total over a half million. This is a loosely structured group that may be roughly divided into booted eagles and hawk eagles. As their name implies, hawk eagles tend to be somewhat smaller than other eagles and somewhat more agile.

The final group, serpent and snake eagles, is made up of about fifteen species and is confined to Europe, Asia, and Africa. As their name denotes, these eagles feed primarily on snakes, not excluding the most deadly venomous species. Although they are not immune to venom, they are agile and protected by a thick covering of feathers seldom penetrated by the fangs of serpents. Most have short talons suitable for gripping the slender bodies of snakes; one, in fact, is called the short-toed eagle. Serpent and snake eagles are, as a group, somewhat smaller than most of the eagles of the other three groups, but they are still larger than other raptors. The African bateleur, one of the most colorful eagles, is included in this group.

extraordinarily difficult to study because they nest high up in the largest rainforest trees, often more than 100 feet (30 meters) above the forest floor, and feed mostly on monkeys, sloths, civets, and other arboreal mammals. They seldom descend below the rainforest canopy. Moreover, their proportionately short wings are not well suited for soaring; they usually hunt by flying just above the canopy, and, given the denseness of rainforest foliage, are often invisible from the ground. Large rainforest eagles are found in Latin America and in the Asian Pacific Rim.

The largest eagle group is called the true, or booted, group and comprises more than

In this volume, you will meet a substantial selection of eagle species arranged geographically from the most familiar North American eagles to some of the more obscure but fascinating eagles of South America, the Pacific Rim, and the Old World.

The changeable hawk eagle is a small member of the booted eagle family found in India and much of Southeast Asia.

The African bateleur is among the most colorful of the serpent-eating eagles.

NORTH AMERICA

After Antarctica, which has no breeding eagles at all, North America is the most "eagle poor" of the continents with respect to variety of species. A few South and Central American eagles range as far north as southern Mexico, and Steller's sea eagles and white-tailed eagles sometimes wander into Alaska. Essentially, however, North America has only two native species, the bald, or American, eagle and the golden eagle.

On the other hand, North America is quite well supplied with respect to total population of birds in general. Current estimates for Canada and the United States including Alaska place the number of golden eagles at more than 100,000 and the number of bald eagles at more than 50,000. In the lower forty-eight states there are probably at least fifty thousand golden eagles and twelve thousand bald eagles. Both species are widely distributed, although the golden eagle is much more common in the West than in the East, and both are currently increasing in population.

Bald Eagles

In 1782, by act of Congress, the bald eagle was chosen to adorn the Great Seal of the United States and hence became our national bird. Benjamin Franklin led the loyal minority in championing the turkey. He pointed out that the bald eagle was an unscrupulous opportunist who stole the prey of other birds, ate raw fish, and scavenged on carrion, and was of no known benefit to mankind, whereas the turkey was the most succulent of fowls. Some still argue that modern politics is better symbolized by the turkey than the eagle, but Franklin lost, and the bald eagle officially became the American eagle.

The bald eagle is a member of the sea and fish eagle family. Among the largest of the eagles, it breeds only in North America. A fully grown adult will have a length of about 3 feet (.92 meter) and a wingspan of 7 to 8 feet (2.14 to 2.44 meters); it will weigh from ten to fourteen pounds. Wild bald eagles may live as long as thirty years, but the average

The sharp, hooked talons and thick, powerful beak of the bald eagle are typical of sea eagles, which subsist primarily on fish.

Bald eagles nest in tall trees near rivers, lakes, or ocean coasts.

lifespan is probably about fifteen to twenty years. They normally mate for life, but when one member of the pair dies, the survivor will not hesitate to accept a new mate. Bald eagles nest in large trees near rivers or coasts and will often use and rebuild the same nest year after year. Some nests eventually acquire gigantic proportions, as much as 9 feet (2.75 meters) in diameter with a weight of two tons; a typical nest is about 5 feet (1.53 meters) in diameter. In this nest the female eagle will usually lay two eggs which will hatch in about thirty-five days. Sometimes two chicks will survive, but it is not uncommon for the older eaglet to kill the smaller one. In healthy habitats a pair of bald eagles will produce an average of 1.5 surviving offspring each year. The eaglets are able to leave the nest and begin hunting on their own after about three months.

Bald eagles are perched atop a very long food chain and are particularly vulnerable to some kinds of environmental pollution. In the twenty years immediately following World War II, the population of bald eagles in the lower forty-eight states dropped alarmingly. It became apparent that our national bird was on the verge of extinction everywhere except Alaska, where no decline was observed. By 1965, only about four hundred breeding pairs remained in the lower forty-eight states, and perhaps as few as forty of those were successfully hatching and rearing young. Another alarming sign was that the percentage of immature birds observed in the wild was much lower than it had traditionally been.

The same nesting site may be used for many years. Eagles add to the nest of sticks each year until it becomes quite large, as much as 9 feet (2.75 meters) in diameter.

It has been reported but not confirmed that before leaving the nest, a bald eagle will cover its eggs by dragging nest lining material over them.

These bald eagle hatchlings, covered with light gray down, are less than two weeks of age.

Sometimes only one eaglet is raised to maturity, particularly when the parent birds have difficulty locating food.

Since the banning of DDT, the nesting success of bald eagles has increased dramatically. It is not unusual for a single nest to produce two surviving eaglets.

The call of the bald eagle is a gull-like screech, harsh and broken.

A number of factors were recognized as contributing to the decline of the bald eagle. Loss of habitat was an obvious one, since eagles do not usually nest in areas where there is a lot of human activity. Also, some eagles were still being shot, even though they were officially protected by federal law. In Alaska—in response to pressure from the salmon industry and the fur trade—there was actually a bounty on bald eagles from 1917 until 1953. During this period, the Alaska Territory paid cash for about 125,000 dead bald eagles.

The main culprit in the decline of bald eagles, however, was identified in 1959 by Rachel Carson in her landmark book, *Silent Spring.* It was pesticides, particularly DDT. DDT is long lived and tends to become concentrated in the fatty tissues of animals and fish exposed to it. The concentration increases as one moves up the food chain. A minnow feeding on mayflies contaminated with DDT will be eaten by a small fish which will in turn be eaten by a larger fish; eventually, the DDT will be concentrated in types of large, oily fish such as spawning salmon, which are preferred by bald eagles.

For the most part, bald eagles are not actually killed by ingesting fish contaminated with DDT unless the pesticide is very highly

concentrated. Rather, they continue to behave in normal fashion and even go through normal mating and nest-building cycles. It is here, however, that the effects of the pesticide become visible. When the female bird attempts to lay her eggs, they may immediately break. Or they may break at some point during the incubation period. The most serious effect of DDT on the reproductive cycles of eagles is the reduction of eggshell thickness to the point that few eggs survive unbroken long enough to actually produce eaglets.

Recognition of this problem was one of the main reasons that DDT was banned by the federal government in 1972, a step that had already been taken by several states, including my home state of Michigan. It was recognized at that time that the bald eagle was in dire

straits, and that more than one action would be needed to bring it back from the brink of extinction. The federal Endangered Species Program took steps to preserve and restore traditional eagle habitats and began more rigorous enforcement of laws prohibiting the harming of eagles and the possession of eagle parts, particularly feathers. When it became apparent that some eagles were dying from lead poisoning as a result of ingesting ducks that had been wounded by hunters or had inadvertently swallowed lead shot, a ban on lead shot was proposed and eventually implemented, beginning in 1991.

Biologists discovered that they could remove eggs from eagles' nests and that the eagles would lay new eggs. Eggs thus gathered were used in a captive breeding program at the United States Fish and Wildlife Service's

Where coastal trees are unavailable, as in the Aleutians, bald eagles build their nests on high promontories.

Patuxent Wildlife Research Center in Maryland. As the hatchlings matured, some were retained as breeding stock, but most were used to reestablish bald eagles in areas such as New England, where there was plenty of good habitat but where DDT had totally extirpated the remnant population.

During the 1970s, the outlook remained gloomy because DDT is a persistent chemical; the mere banning of its use did not immediately remove it from the environment. Also, since eagles don't begin to breed until they are about five years old, all of the eagles breeding during the mid-1970s had been hatched before the DDT ban went into effect. By the late 1970s and early 1980s, however, progress began to be noticeable. By the late 1980s, the recovery of the American bald eagle was considered one of the major environmental miracles of the twentieth century. There was at least a tenfold increase in the population of wild bald eagles in the lower forty-eight states between 1972 and 1988, when the Patuxent program of captive rearing was terminated because it was no longer needed. By 1994, the recovery had progressed so well that the bald eagle was removed from the list of endangered species in all but a few

A mature bald eagle preening its feathers.

Bald eagles mate for life and share the duties of caring for their offspring.

states and was reclassified as "threatened," a much less critical designation.

This does not mean that vigilance is no longer needed to ensure the preservation of the species. New problems continue to arise as the old ones are solved. For example, in the winter of 1994–95 at DeGray Lake in Arkansas, bald eagles began dying mysteriously: twenty-nine in all. The cause of the deaths was unknown, but all of the dead eagles had been feeding on coots, the population of which also suffered an unexplained die-off apparently caused by some toxin.

Whatever the cause, biologists were relieved the following winter to find that the die-off did not recur. But it did happen again in 1996–97, and the cause is still not known.

Today, bald eagles are found in all states except Hawaii. Michigan, with its endless miles of Great Lakes shoreline, has over 250 active nests, as opposed to fewer than thirty in the early 1970s. And where I saw no eagles at all in Michigan until 1982, I currently see several each year in such places as the Straits of Mackinaw, Whitefish Point, Seney National Wildlife Refuge, and Grand Marais. Seeing our national bird restored to its traditional haunts certainly adds depth to the Great Lakes experience.

People who would like to see more than the scattered few eagles typical in most of the nation can easily do so if they are willing to travel. The greatest concentration of bald eagles on the continent occurs in November and December on the Chilkat River near Haines, Alaska. The 49,000-acre Alaska Chilkat Bald Eagle Preserve was established there in 1982 on the two hundredth anniversary of the selection of the bald eagle as our national bird. Salmon runs are common throughout Alaska and British Columbia, but the run of chum salmon on the Chilkat is both highly concentrated (from 200,000 to 500,000 fish) and late in the year. The result is that—in the case of one tagged bird—bald eagles come from as far away as the Willapa National Wildlife Refuge in the state of

An eagle protects its food by partially opening its wings, or tenting.

A bald eagle raises its wings and assumes a threatening pose to defend its meal.

Washington, 1,100 miles (1,770 kilometers) to the south, to gorge themselves against the lean pickings of the winter. Between three and four thousand birds gather annually in about a 10-mile (16-kilometer) stretch of the Chilkat. Observers report being able to count one thousand eagles at one time by standing in a single open location and slowly turning 360 degrees while looking through binoculars.

Even when the salmon aren't running, the Haines area is a good place to see eagles; there are about a hundred active nests within a few miles of town. I can recall walking along the Haines waterfront in July with my daughter Laura (who is the best eagle spotter I have ever known) and seeing several eagles in town, perched on power poles and dock pilings. And similar, if smaller, concentrations of eagles occur in southeastern Alaska and British Columbia at several spots where there are dependable annual salmon runs.

Alaska is, of course, a long way to go for someone who would just like to see some eagles. Probably the best alternative is the

Following page: Until recently, concentrations of bald eagles like this were found only in Alaska. Now, similar gatherings occur each winter in the upper Mississippi valley.

23

*A bald eagle
extends its legs
far forward
as it prepares
to snare a fish.*

*The eagle impales
a fish by quickly
snapping its
talons to the rear.*

Once it has secured the fish, the eagle flaps its powerful wings to lift its prey from the water.

The eagle carries its fish with its talons as it flies to a nearby perch.

Bald eagles engage in a variety of courtship flights which may include locking talons and descending in a series of somersaults.

northern Mississippi valley during January and February. Before the banning of DDT, this area was almost bereft of eagles, but not any more. As many as five thousand bald eagles winter on the river between Cairo, Illinois, and St. Paul, Minnesota, tending to concentrate near several large dams. Communities in the area have learned that preserving their eagle populations can be profitable. By hosting eagle festivals, they are able to attract a significant influx of tourists at a time of year when tourism was traditionally nonexistent. In a typical January, one may attend the Quad Cities Bald Eagle Days in Rock Island, Illinois, the Dubuque Bald Eagle Watch in Dubuque, Iowa, the Clinton Bald Eagle Watch in Clinton, Iowa, the Keokuk Bald Eagle Days in Keokuk, Iowa, the LeClaire Bald Eagle Watch in LeClaire, Wisconsin, and the Muscatine Bald Eagle Watch in Muscatine, Iowa. For those who go south for the winter, Emory, Texas, hosts a January Eagle Fest with a juried art exhibition and barge tours of lakes where eagles gather.

The extended legs indicate that this bald eagle is preparing either to land or to dive upon a fish it has spotted while cruising at a typical hunting altitude.

Settled on its perch, the eagle prepares to enjoy its meal.

Golden Eagle

America's other eagle, the golden eagle, is neither as well known nor as highly revered as the bald eagle. Lacking the distinctive white head and tail of the latter, it is not as easily recognized. It is usually seen from a distance, soaring on thermals against a bright sky, and appears to be black, although its typical coloration is actually dark brown. It may easily be mistaken for the common turkey vulture, which it superficially resembles, but the golden eagle soars on relatively flat wings, while the wings of the turkey vulture curve upward. The golden tipped feathers on the crown and nape of the neck that give the eagle its name are not visible from a distance of more than a

North American golden eagles prefer the rugged terrain of the Rocky Mountains and the high prairie.

few feet. However, the golden eagle is in no respect a less noble creature than its more famous counterpart; it even has some claims to superiority.

In size, golden eagles are comparable to, but perhaps slightly smaller than, bald eagles. They have a length of about 3 feet (.92 meters), a wingspan of 6 to 7 feet (1.83 to 2.14 meters), and a weight of eight to thirteen pounds. Like bald eagles, they usually mate for life, (about fifteen to twenty years), reach sexual maturity at the age of four or five years, and annually incubate a clutch of two eggs, which hatch in thirty-five to forty-five days, and from which one or occasionally two eaglets are reared. The eaglets are mature enough to leave the nest in about three and a half months.

Here, the similarities to bald eagles end. Golden eagles are not fish eaters and do not congregate near water. They prefer the Rocky

The golden-tipped feathers which contrast with the mostly dark brown plumage of an adult golden eagle are clearly visible only at close range.

31

Mountains and the high prairies of such states as Montana, Wyoming, and Colorado. Their nests, true examples of aeries, are often constructed on high rock outcroppings. Some sites have been in continuous use for many years, perhaps centuries. One nest on a high bluff near the Sun River in Montana is reported to be 21 feet high (6.4 meters) and still growing. As a rule, golden eagles tend to spread out more than bald eagles because they prey on land animals, which do not gather in "schools," like fish.

A golden eagle pair will establish a territory of twelve to eighteen thousand acres—about 25 square miles (65 square kilometers)—and will defend it against all avian intruders. An example of the territoriality of golden eagles caused a small setback for the California condor recovery program.

Condors are the largest North American raptors, having (at adulthood) a length of 4 1/2 feet (1.37 meters), a wingspan of over 9 feet (2.75 meters), and a weight of more than twenty pounds. They are about fifty percent larger than golden eagles. On the brink of extinction, the remaining wild California condors were captured, and a captive breeding program was initiated. The intent was to eventually reintroduce the birds to current condor habitat in California, and also to establish new populations in other areas where condors had been known to live in historic times. By 1996, the captive population had increased to the point at which biologists felt it was time to establish a new condor range in Grand Canyon National Park. Six birds were released there.

Five of the introduced condors remained in the general vicinity of where they were released and were doing fine in early 1997. The sixth strayed into the territory of a pair of golden eagles, where it was promptly attacked and killed by one of the smaller birds.

Golden eagles are the most widely distributed of all the eagle species. They breed throughout the northern hemisphere north of the Tropic of Cancer; in much of the world, when one says "eagle," one is referring to the golden eagle. The tawny eagle and steppe eagle of Europe, Africa, and Asia, and the Australian wedge-tailed eagle might possibly have larger populations, but this is difficult to determine because the golden eagle is so widely distributed that no very accurate estimate of its population is possible. In North and Central America, its population is thought to be about 200,000, with about 65,000 birds resident in the lower forty-eight states. The most conservative worldwide estimates place the total population of golden eagles at more than a half million. It is clear that the golden eagle is the least endangered of all eagle species and that it is currently increasing in many places, including the United States and the British Isles.

During the DDT scare of the 1970s, alarms were raised about the status of the golden eagle in the United States. One estimate suggested that its numbers were dwindling to fewer than ten thousand birds, and that it would soon suffer the same catastrophe as that affecting bald eagles. However, a study conducted shortly thereafter concluded that more than ten thousand golden eagles were

A golden eagle uses its long wings to discourage its prey from darting past it. Although they prey mainly on small mammals like rabbits and squirrels, they have been known to attack and kill animals as large as young sheep and antelope.

Many of the animals upon which golden eagles prey are found in the high meadows of the American West. Golden Eagles are the most widely distributed eagle species in the world.

Golden eagles prey primarily on small mammals such as rabbits or squirrels.

alive and well in the state of Montana alone. Golden eagles prey primarily on vegetable-eating mammals and, at times, birds of the prairie and mountains. They like jackrabbits, ground squirrels and prairie dogs, marmots, grouse, and, unfortunately for their reputation, lambs. Hence, golden eagles were totally unaffected by the reproductive damage from DDT that had such a severe impact on bald eagles and peregrine falcons.

Golden eagles routinely kill jackrabbits, which far outweigh them. In the believe-it-or-not category, one observer (reputed to have been sober) reports having seen a golden eagle dive on a young antelope and embed its talons in the animal's throat. The antelope struggled for several minutes, but eventually collapsed and died from loss of blood. The twelve-pound eagle then began feeding on the carcass of the seventy-pound antelope.

One of the legendary enmities of the West has been that of the sheep rancher against the golden eagle. If sheep ranchers have overstated the damage done to their flocks by eagles, it is equally clear that conservationists have understated it. Golden eagles can at times become a serious problem. Jackrabbits and other hares have cyclical population patterns. When they are increasing, animals and birds which prey on them also increase. When the population of jackrabbits crashes, as it always will at some point, a lot of bobcats, coyotes, and eagles are left with little to eat. At such times, they may kill a substantial percentage of newborn lambs in a given region. For the most part, however, eagle depredation is limited to lambs of less than two months of age and occurs at a significant level only when jackrabbits are scarce. At other times, eagles prefer their traditional prey to ranch-bred domestic stock.

There is good news for the eagle in North America. The golden eagle continues to thrive and increase, and the bald eagle has come back from the brink of extinction to become almost commonplace in some parts of its range. With continued vigilance, there is no reason to doubt that both eagles will grace our countryside throughout the twenty-first century.

Unfortunately, the grassland habitat preferred by golden eagles is also excellent for raising sheep. Sheep ranchers have traditionally opposed measures protecting eagles.

Golden eagles may nest in trees like bald eagles, or may nest on high rock ledges. A pair of golden eagles will aggressively protect their territory from any avian intruders.

SOUTH AMERICA AND THE PACIFIC RIM

Like North America, South America has a relatively limited variety of eagle species: only eight. It has no sea eagles and no serpent-eating eagles. However, four of the world's six species of large rainforest eagles, including the legendary harpy eagle, are native to South and Central America. Latin America is also home to four members of the group known as booted eagles, including the ornate hawk eagle, considered by many to be the world's most beautiful eagle.

Central and South America

The premier eagle of Central and South America is the magnificent harpy, whose range extends from southern Mexico to northern Argentina. A female harpy, typically about a third larger than the male, is the largest New World eagle; she is 3 1/2 feet (1.06 meters) in length, has a wingspan of 6 to 6 1/2 feet (1.83 to 1.98 meters), and weighs nearly twenty pounds. The head of the harpy has a distinctive cowl of blackish, white-tipped feathers lengthening into a large divided crest, which gives the eagle a wild, somewhat disheveled appearance thought to be reminiscent of the harpy of classical mythology, a predatory monster with the head of a woman and the body and claws of a vulture. However frightening this bird may appear to be, and although it is a true predator and not usually a carrion eater, there is no indication that it is any more ferocious than other large eagles. Its call has been described as much softer than one would expect to come from a bird of this magnitude.

Instead of soaring on thermals like bald or golden eagles, harpies tend to cruise just above the top of the rainforest canopy seek-

The long divided crest feathers of the South American harpy eagle give the bird a wild, disheveled appearance.

ing prey that is itself primarily arboreal. Occasionally a harpy may dive below the canopy to kill a snake or a ground rodent such as an agouti, but mostly it preys on howler monkeys, squirrel monkeys, two- and three-toed sloths, kinkajous, tree porcupines, and tamanduas, all of which live high up in the tops of trees. If it is breeding, it will deliver its kill to a four- or five-foot diameter nest, usually built in a gigantic silk-cotton tree at a level of between 110 and 160 feet (30.5 to 48.8 meters). Characteristically, the harpy lays two eggs but raises only one eaglet; as soon as that eaglet hatches (about eight weeks after the egg is laid), the female eagle stops incubating the second egg. Six months or so later, the young harpy eagle is mature enough to leave the nest.

Studying the harpy eagle is among the most difficult and, at times, most dangerous tasks undertaken by field ornithologists. The normal behavior of the harpy makes it almost impossible for observers to locate it away from the nest. Observations of hunting harpies making kills have occurred by accident when ornithologists studying some other rainforest species have happened to be in the right place at the right time. And it is not unusual for a biologist who has worked in harpy country for many years to report

White-bellied sea eagles are widespread in coastal south Asia, Indonesia, and Australia.

only three or four such encounters. Fortunately for observers, however, harpy nests are relatively conspicuous and are often used for several seasons. The obvious problem, of course, is that the observer can see very little looking straight up from a distance of perhaps 150 feet (45.75 meters); therefore, tree climbing is a necessary skill for anyone studying this species.

Researchers select a tall but climbable tree adjacent to the nest tree and attempt to build a blind at a level a few feet higher than the nest. They try to minimize human impact on the lives of the birds by doing most of their construction work while the adult eagles are off hunting. However, harpies always become aware of the intruders and, even so, do not abandon their nest or their eaglet. What they do is attack. Imagine what is like to be climbing a flimsy rope ladder toward a blind more than 100 feet (30 meters) above the forest floor when you are dived upon by a twenty-pound female eagle with talons longer than the claws of a grizzly bear. Harpy researchers make their observations while wearing motorcycle helmets, bulletproof vests, and thick leather jackets in one-hundred-degree equatorial heat and rainforest humidity. Many of them still suffer minor injuries from talon punctures where the armor isn't thick enough, or more serious injuries from falls.

Despite the heroic efforts of researchers, the status of the harpy eagle is obscure. Obviously, slash-and-burn depletion of rainforests is rapidly and alarmingly reducing the traditional habitat of this magnificent raptor. However, harpies seem relatively well distributed in the remaining habitat and that habitat is still substantial; it is doubtful that this eagle is in immediate danger. On the other hand, one disturbing trend is the disappearance of harpies from former nesting grounds in Central America, where much rainforest remains and where their prey is abundant. Costa Rica, for example, has set aside large tracts of rainforest and cloud forest as nature preserves, but has still lost its harpy eagles. An increase in human activities would seem to be the most likely explanation.

Somewhat smaller relatives of the harpy are the crested eagle, solitary eagle, and crowned solitary eagle, which occupy South and Central American rainforests. In addition, four members of the booted eagle family, including the ornate hawk eagle, breed in Latin America. The ornate hawk eagle is less than a third of the weight of the harpy. It has a length of 2 feet (.61 meters) and a wingspan of less than 4 feet. Many observers, however, consider it to be the most beautiful of all the eagles. It has a long, pointed black crest above a black crown, a nape and shoulders of rich chestnut, a pure white breast, and alternating

The crowned hawk eagle is distinguished by a prominent black-tipped double crest.

Harpy eagles are stocky birds with powerful legs and unusually long talons.

The white-bellied sea eagle is the slimmest and most graceful of the fish-eating eagles.

Wedge-tailed eagles spend part of each day on perches, watching for hares and rabbits which are their preferred food.

The black-and-chestnut eagle of the Andes Mountains is the only large South American booted eagle.

the Asian counterpart of the harpy eagle; Steller's sea eagle, generally conceded to be the largest of the world's eagles; and the wedge-tailed eagle of Australia, which, with an estimated population of about 700,000, is one of the three most populous eagles.

In the family of sea eagles, the Steller's reigns supreme. It breeds along the eastern coast of Siberia and Korea and winters slightly farther south in a region that includes northern Japan. Although its length approximates that of the bald eagle and harpy eagle—a little over 3 feet (.92 meters)—a female Steller's eagle may have a wingspan in excess of 8 feet (2.44 meters), a weight of twenty pounds, and a 3-inch (7.62 centimeter) beak. The large beak is necessary because these eagles prey on Pacific salmon, which

The beaks of fish-eating eagles like this white-bellied sea eagle tend to be longer and more powerful than those of other types of eagles.

black and white stripes on its legs and tail. The other booted eagles of South and Central America are the black-and-chestnut eagle of the Andes, the black hawk eagle, and the black-and-white hawk eagle.

The Pacific Rim

The region included in this section comprises Australia, the Pacific coast of Asia, and such major island groups as Japan, the Philippines, and the East Indies. This is a particularly rich area for eagles, and the only area that contains species representing all four major eagle groups. No fewer than twenty-three species regularly occur in this region; six of these are found throughout much of mainland Asia and are included in the chapter on Old World eagles, and one is the golden eagle found throughout the northern hemisphere and profiled in the chapter on North American eagles.

The remaining sixteen species are most impressive. Among them are the Philippine eagle, a very large rainforest raptor, which is

The gray eagle buzzard is found in open country and dry woodlands throughout most of South America.

have very tough hides. They also, however, may eat ptarmigan, ducks and geese, hares, sables, foxes, young seals, shellfish, and carrion.

Like other sea eagles, Steller's tend to nest in large coastal trees, reusing the same nests year after year, building them up to the point that nests 8 feet (2.44 meters) across and 12 feet (3.66 meters) thick are not uncommon. And, like bald eagles, Steller's tend to congregate where there are major salmon runs. This is, however, a much rarer eagle; it probably has a total population of fifteen to twenty thousand, with four to five thousand mature breeding pairs. Fortunately, this small population seems to be stable, and the Steller's sea eagle is not considered threatened.

Other sea eagles found along the Pacific Rim include the white-bellied sea eagle, which is widely distributed and ranges as far west as the coast of India; Sanford's sea eagle, which lives only in the Solomon Islands and is among the least known eagles; and the small gray-headed fishing eagle of the Asian coast and the East Indies.

Two large rainforest eagles, including the spectacular Philippine eagle, live in this region. Until the 1970s, the Philippine eagle was known as the "monkey-eating eagle," but the name was changed because ornithologists conclusively demonstrated that, although monkeys, deer, and cobras make up a small part of the eagle's diet, it feeds primarily on flying lemurs. It closely resembles the harpy eagle and is nearly as large, reaching seventeen and a half pounds in weight. Sadly, human population expansion in the Philippines has all but eliminated the old-growth rainforests that are the habitat of the Philippine eagle, and the bird is severely endangered. At most, two hundred birds survive on Mindinao, Samar, Luzon, and Leyte, and that is probably an optimistic estimate. Rainforest destruction continues unabated at a rate that will bring about the loss of all Philippine eagle habitat in less than ten years. At that time, the

The huge Philippine eagle is considered the Asian counterpart to the harpy. Loss of habitat has brought it to the brink of extinction.

Philippine eagle will exist only in zoos. Fortunately, habitat destruction is not yet a serious problem in New Guinea, where the other Pacific rainforest eagle, the New Guinea eagle, resides. But this rare eagle has been seldom observed, and little is known of its behavior or status.

At least seven booted eagles are found in this region, among them the major eagle of

Young white-bellied sea eagles remain in the nest and are tended to by both parents for about nine or ten weeks after hatching.

Like other sea eagles, the white-bellied sea eagle usually builds a large nest of sticks high in a tree near water.

plays, diving, swooping, and even looping the loop. Their large nests are similar to those of bald eagles and are built 20 to 40 feet (6.1 to 12.2 meters) above the ground in trees. The female normally lays two eggs and raises one or two eaglets.

The other booted eagles of the Pacific include the little eagle of Australia, a small, stocky bird that also feeds primarily on rabbits, and several island-dwelling hawk eagles. Among these is the Javan hawk eagle, which, due to loss of rainforest habitat, has been reduced to no more than sixty pairs; it may be the world's rarest eagle.

Finally, the region has at least three species of serpent eagles, most notable of which is the crested serpent eagle. Depending on whether the various forms of this eagle are considered subspecies or separate species, there may be one or as many as five species of crested serpent eagles. These are primarily forest birds that, as their name implies, feed mostly on snakes (especially tree-climbing snakes), although they also eat lizards and some small mammals. They tend to hunt from perches in thick forests. They have short, thick toes adapted to grasping and killing slender snakes, and, as is typical of most snake and serpent eagles, they have large yellow eyes. Crested serpent eagles and others in this group, such as the Philippine serpent eagle and Celebes serpent eagle, thrive in the snake-infested islands of tropical east Asia.

Wedge-tailed eagles soar to great heights, sometimes becoming almost invisible to the human eye.

Australia, known as the wedge-tailed eagle. It is one of the larger booted eagles, with a length of 3 feet (.92 meters), a wing span of 7 feet (2.14 meters), and a weight approaching twelve pounds. The normal range of this eagle includes only the continent of Australia and the island of Tasmania. Even though it has been targeted as a pest by sheep ranchers, the wedge-tailed eagle has the good fortune of preferring rabbits as its staple dinner. Rabbits, having few other natural enemies in Australia, are more than abundant, and this means that the wedge-tailed eagle is also abundant.

During breeding season, wedge-tailed eagles put on spectacular aerial courtship dis-

The wedge-tailed eagle, a handsome member of the booted eagle family, is the most common eagle of inland Australia.

A pair of white-bellied eagles surveys their surroundings from a tree perch in Australia.

EUROPE, CONTINENTAL ASIA, AND AFRICA

Europe

At the time of Shakespeare, eagles were not especially uncommon in the British Isles and northern Europe. There were two main species: the golden eagle and the white-tailed fish eagle also known as the erne. Both eventually came to be thought of as threats to livestock and game and were relentlessly persecuted to the degree that they were almost totally eliminated. In England, the last breeding pair of white-tailed fish eagles was shot in 1916; one unpaired female survived until 1918, but after that the erne was extinct in Great Britain. As explained in chapter one, the golden eagle likes high, craggy country; it was not completely wiped out in the British Isles, but was reduced to a tiny remnant population in the Scottish Highlands. And both species suffered similar persecution from gamekeepers and livestock farmers on the continent.

In the final quarter of the twentieth century, a 180-degree change in the northern

The European counterpart to the bald eagle is the white-tailed sea eagle, or erne.

The golden eagle, named for the golden-tipped feathers on its head, neck, and shoulders, is not confined to North America, but also inhabits much of northern Europe and Asia.

The white-tailed sea eagle was nearly exterminated in much of its range early in this century, but it is now being reestablished in England and northern Europe.

The booted eagle is a relatively small woodland bird of southern Europe, northern Africa, and southern Asia. Its plumage somewhat resembles that of the American red-tailed hawk.

Imperial eagles have been used as symbols of royalty since the time of the pharaohs. They breed across southern Europe and Asia as far east as India, and migrate to northern Africa in winter.

European attitude toward eagles has occurred. Fortunately, the destruction of local populations of white-tailed sea eagles and golden eagles did not threaten either species with extinction because both have very large ranges that include nearly all of northern Asia and, in the case of the golden eagle, North America also. Norway, which hosted about 350 breeding pairs of white-tailed sea eagles, led the movement to preserve and increase eagle populations in the early 1970s. By 1975, England had begun to protect its remaining golden eagles and was importing white-tailed sea eagles from Norway in an attempt to reestablish a breeding population. This attempt has, so far, met with less than ideal success. Over one hundred Norwegian birds have been released, but there are currently only about ten known breeding pairs. Golden eagles have fared somewhat better and increased to perhaps 450 pairs, mostly in Scotland and the harsh, thinly populated North Sea islands.

Two related booted eagles, the greater spotted eagle and the lesser spotted eagle, inhabit

central and eastern Europe. Both are small- to moderate-sized dark brown birds that migrate to Africa or tropical Europe in winter. Lesser spotted eagles travel as far south as Mozambique, and substantial numbers of them may be observed as they pass through Israel on their way south in September and back north in March.

Among the eagles of southern Europe, the imperial eagle and the Spanish imperial eagle dominate. These are the eagles whose like- nesses have adorned the crowns of emperors and the staffs of generals since the rise of the pharaohs. Until recently, the Spanish imperial eagle was considered a subspecies of the impe- rial eagle, but it has now been reclassified as a separate species; it is severely threatened, with a total population of perhaps 150 pairs. Both species of imperial eagles are large representa- tives of the booted eagle family. They grow to a length of just under 3 feet (.92 meters), have a wingspan approaching 7 feet (2.14 meters), and weigh about 8 pounds. They breed across southern Europe and Asia as far east as India and migrate to northern Africa, particularly Egypt and the Sudan in winter.

When two golden eagle eggs hatch, the elder eaglet kills the younger, and only one offspring is raised to maturity.

Four other species of booted eagles occur in southern Europe but are more accurately classified as African or Asian birds. These are Bonelli's eagle, the booted eagle, the tawny eagle, and the steppe eagle. The latter two are sometimes considered a single species, and if so, together they become the only eagle species in the world with a population estimated to exceed one million. The Bonelli's, tawny, and steppe eagle are medium-sized, whereas the booted eagle is quite small. All four migrate to the tropics during winter.

Europe also has one resident species of serpent eagle, although it also resides in Asia and is probably most populous in Africa. This is the short-toed eagle, also known as the black-breasted harrier eagle or Beaudouin's harrier eagle. It is a relatively large eagle that prefers plains and deserts. Although serpent eagles usually hunt from tree perches, the short-toed eagle spends most of its time in the air, not soaring high on thermals, but cruising less than 100 feet (30 meters) above the ground. Most of its diet consists of snakes. In fact, these eagles are so focused on snakes that in captivity they will ignore dead mammals or birds but will attack a rope twitched through their cage. The short-toed eagle kills by grasping a snake's body firmly with its short, stubby toes and mutilating the snake's head with its beak.

The short-toed eagle is the only snake-eating eagle native to Europe.

A substantial portion of the tawny eagle's diet consists of carrion, for which it competes with vultures.

53

The steppe eagle is a close relative of the tawny eagle. At one time the two eagles were considered to be different color phases of the same species.

Following page: The tawny eagle is considered to be among the most populous of all the world's eagles.

In addition to eating carrion, tawny eagles also prey on small mammals, lizards, and snakes.

The plumage of the tawny eagle varies greatly. This adult exhibits the golden brown color that gives the eagle its name.

Africa

The continent of Africa is blessed with both a large variety and large populations of eagles. Those factors that have reduced eagle numbers elsewhere—pollution, persecution by ranchers and gamekeepers, and loss of habitat—have as of yet not played a significant role in Africa. It is obvious that, in comparison to the predation by the great cats and crocodiles and hyenas and wild dogs, the damage to game species by eagle predation is no cause for worry. Moreover, attempts made to protect Africa's spectacular and unique large mammals such as elephants, lions, and rhinos have included the setting aside of vast tracts of land in national parks. Ecotourism has become a significant part of the economy of several African nations, so the park system is likely to continue growing. And although eagles are not identified as targets of these programs, they certainly are its beneficiaries. Significant sections of eagle habitat are being preserved, and the various populations of fish, snakes, small mammals, and birds upon which African eagles prey are being sustained.

In addition to the eight African species of eagles that also occur in Europe and have already been identified, Africa has fifteen species that are either exclusive to the continent or found only in Africa and the Middle East. These comprise three fish eagles, six snake or serpent eagles, and six booted eagles.

The tawny eagle surveys the terrain of the Masai Mara in Kenya from a typical perch in an Acacia tree.

The long-crested eagle is a small but easily recognizable eagle that inhabits much of Africa south of the Sahara.

The black-chested snake eagle is a close relative of the European short-toed eagle. It inhabits mostly open or lightly wooded country in eastern Africa from the Sudan to South Africa.

Both male and female crowned hawk eagles of Africa share in the building of impressively large nests, and both also incubate their eggs.

Like most snake eagles, the black-chested snake eagle spends most of its time watching for prey from a perch rather than in flight.

Among the fish eagles are two that are particularly worthy of attention. One is the African fish eagle, a handsome bird that in both size and plumage closely resembles the bald eagle, except that the white on the head extends to the shoulders and upper breast. These are the eagles most typically seen by tourists in the Lake Victoria region and the ones usually shown in documentary television programs on African wildlife. Like bald eagles, they gather in significant numbers where there are concentrations of fish. Probably no eagle except the bald eagle has been so thoroughly studied or as frequently filmed as the African fish eagle. Leslie Brown, one of the great eagle researchers of the century, devoted his life to studying this species.

The other African fish eagle of note is the vulturine fish eagle, the most peculiar of all eagles, if it indeed is an eagle—and that is in some doubt. It certainly looks like an eagle, particularly around the head, which, although it has some bare skin like a vulture, has that classic regal shape that decorates coins and coats of arms. But its alternate name is the palm nut vulture. And it quacks like a duck when it isn't growling like a dog or

Silhouetted against the setting sun is the most studied and most photographed of all African eagles, the African fish eagle.

About ninety percent of the diet of the African fish eagle is made up of fish, particularly catfish and lungfish. It also preys on such water birds as storks, herons, spoonbills, and flamingos.

African fish eagles are common on most of east Africa's large inland lakes. This eagle is carrying a fish just above the surface of Lake Baringo in Kenya.

The African fish eagle is similar in appearance to the bald eagle, but the white on its head extends well down onto its back and chest.

The Madagascar serpent-eagle is a very rare forest eagle which is seldom observed and about which little is known.

Although it is classified as a snake eagle, the bateleur has a varied diet made up partly of reptiles but also of small mammals such as rats, hedgehogs, squirrels, and hares.

With its red face, black ruff, brown back, and gray wingpatch, the bateleur of Africa is one of the world's most colorful eagles.

cat. Its most unbelievable characteristic, however, is that it is a vegetarian. Not only is it the only vegetarian eagle, it is the only species out of the world's hundreds of birds classified as raptors that has given up the eating of meat. It is called a raptor because it possesses all the physical characteristics—strong bill, keen eyesight, sharp talons, and large size—necessary to be a successful predator. It simply prefers not to. At some point it developed a taste for the nuts of the oil palm which contain about as much saturated fat as the flesh of the oily fish that it once preyed upon. Now it uses its strong feet to walk up sloping palm branches while it gobbles nuts with its powerful predatory beak.

Two other African eagles are of note because of their spectacular appearance. The first is a serpent eagle called the bateleur. Its range covers nearly all of Africa south of the Sahara. For the most part, the plumage of the bateleur is black and shaggy, but there are striking light brown patches topped with white on the wings. Both the face and feet of a bateleur are bright red. In proportion to the rest of its dimensions, its wings are so long and wide that it has been called the prototype for the airplane wing, and it spends nearly all of its waking hours soaring.

The second is the martial eagle, a member of the booted eagle family. This is the largest African eagle, with a length just under 3 feet (.92 meters), a wingspan of nearly 7 feet (2.14 meters), and a weight of about thirteen pounds. Martial eagles like open plains, semi-desert country, and savannahs, where they feed on a wide variety of large birds and small to medium mammals including some monkeys and the calves of antelope. Unlike many other eagles, martial eagles are not known to eat carrion.

For the birder wishing to see a variety of eagle species, Africa is the place to go. There are several places in Africa where, during the northern winter, an observer can easily record a dozen different eagle species in a single day.

Martial eagles establish territories when nesting but at other times may wander hundreds of miles over savannas, open plains, and semi-desert country.

A martial eagle, the largest of the African Eagles, is shown feeding on the carcass of an antelope it has killed.

Asia

Asia is another continent rich in eagles, but many of the Asian eagles have already been described in sections on the Pacific Rim and Europe and Africa. Including all the species that overlap with other regions, Asia has about thirty species of eagles. The largest is the Steller's sea eagle profiled in the Pacific Rim section, and the most prolific is the steppe eagle included in the section on Europe.

What is left, primarily, is the eagle assortment found in India and nearby countries. Northern India is another of those locations where twelve or more species of eagles may be observed in one day. Among these is Pallas's sea eagle, which prefers inland lakes and rivers, and not oceans as the name denotes. It spends much of its time perched on trees near the water, waiting for a dead fish to float by; it can catch live fish, but it prefers dead ones when they are available.

As would be expected, serpent eagles, including some families of the crested serpent eagle, are common in south Asia, which has more than its share of snakes. Also, India and southeast Asia have a variety of hawk eagles, including the chestnut-bellied hawk eagle, the crested, or changeable, hawk eagle, the mountain, or feather-toed, hawk eagle, and Blyth's hawk eagle.

One strange eagle that doesn't fit neatly in any of the groups but is usually included with the booted eagles is the Indian black eagle. Although these birds have feathered legs, they most closely resemble kites, with wings narrower and more pointed than those typical of eagles. They inhabit steep, heavily wooded country, usually below five thousand feet (1,525 meters) in elevation, and fly very slowly in a circling pattern. They will occasionally prey on small mammals and ground birds, but their primary food is baby birds and birds' eggs. They often grab and remove birds' nests from the forest canopy, then perch somewhere and feed on the contents.

The black eagle is a member of the booted eagle family which inhabits the dry regions of Africa south of the Sudan.

India shares with Africa the distinction of being one of the best places to locate a variety of eagle species in a small area. Not far behind is Israel, where, during the migrations of March and September, as many as eight species may be seen in one day. In the United States, it is difficult to see two species in a day. However, nowhere else in the world is there a concentration of eagles to compare with the gathering of bald eagles on the Chilkat River in Alaska each November.

The prospect for eagles in the twenty-first century is somewhat tenuous but not completely bleak. Almost certainly a few species—including the Philippine eagle and the Javan hawk eagle—will cease to exist, at least as wild birds, and continued slash-and-burn habitat destruction may serious endanger the Harpy and other rainforest eagles. Species with small but stable populations, like the Steller's sea eagle, are not immediately endangered but could become so due to either pollution or habitat destruction. On the positive side, however, some species which suffered sever population reductions during the twentieth century, such as the bald eagle and white-tailed eagle, seemed to have passed the crisis and are currently increasing. And finally, at least three species, the tawney or steppe eagle, the wedge-tailed eagle, and the golden eagle, have such healthy populations that they seem safe for the forseeable future.

The black eagle is not completely black. It has a conspicuous white patch on its back, barely visible in this scene.

The crested or changeable hawk eagle of Southeast Asia is a shy bird of open forests, which hunts by moving from perch to perch rather than by soaring.

INDEX

*Page numbers in **bold-face** type indicate photo captions.*